v v v

Spirit Level

v v v

Karl Christopher Mcclean

v v v

About the Author

Karl Christopher Mcclean was born in Colchester, Essex, U.K. He enjoys hang gliding, parachuting, rock climbing, walking, hiking, cycling, ego/identity dissolving meditation, sharing ideas, reading & writing poetry, and living a balanced healthy lifestyle that boosts his immune system.

Introduction

This is a psychological book to promote self-consciousness. It analyses the necessary balance of security in life - to both feel comfortable and push the boundaries of that comfort. Since security can be manipulated from outside and inside by forces which leave you insecure and in need of security, self-control is the key to freedom.

"WORDS RUN DEEP ENTER YOUR MIND TO FIND THE SOLUTION"

Contents

First Light

First light
Fresh clean breeze
Fog clears
Dew flicks up
Hits my legs
From off my feet.

Coroner and Gravedigger

Coroner and gravedigger
my name engraved into stone
God, I beg to differ.

The Key to Destiny

Words in my head projected onto things,
The way the path was pathed determines what is seen,
A reflection of life changes with dreams.

My Pupils Open Wide

Birds patrol the skies
frogs dive as rain drops ripple ponds
my pupils open wide.

Sea View

Table for two with a sea view
Our dreams meet become one
The horizon constantly moves.

The Buzz in Design

The buzz in design
Hive built to protect our queen
Pollinators seek
Pollen on knees for honey that's—
Derived then stored to survive.

Truth

Serve the most high
As I search no lie
Cycles cycle in the mind
Truths you decide
History stories
Future reveals mysteries
That can open your eye.

The Eternal Gift

A star burning bright
respires life through deep earth roots
the eternal gift.

Brick Walled Orchards

I'm walking through—
brick walled orchards
fed from root$.

Snowball

A snowball augments
declivitous rotation
deliquesce quagmire.

Until I'm Consumed

The depth and width grew
walking around a deluge
until I'm consumed.

Enemy Within Me

Rooted inside me
Feeding concealed thorny
Dependently fiends
Helpless without support
My vulnerability.

Bed of Dreams

Below the world changes
as I sit with these feelings
perched on a bed of dreams.

Uplift

Lifting myself up
Chains strain, BREAK! Fall hit the ground
Steps emerge
Look to the top bound
Physics can't bring me down, lift.

Climbed Euphoria in Decline

Hills recoil
You know how it feels
At the top of a slide.

The climbed euphoria
In decline
Still got to make her mine.

Hit the bottom
Empty inside
Until I make up my mind
Then gravities not on my side.

Sometimes I find myself
Entwined to a vine
Its wine frees me
From denial.

Building Blocks Repair

Moving forwards
Over rocks
That could fracture
Until I peak raptured
But ruptured
Building blocks repair
For next time
The climb will be faster.

Shallow Reflections

Shallow reflections
crystal skies shine as moon tides
fill lagoons too soon.

Die Rise

That rock face I climb
with constant rolling of dice
to fall from great heights.

Walk for Miles

As I pull thoughts out
Carrying my world in a bag
We walk for miles.

Our World on Rails

Staring at stars
I met you on steps
We dance in flames
Out of hopes
The world we built
Through tunnels on rails
Continues to revolve.

Symphony

Hiding behind leaves
little birds up in trees play—
symphonies, for we.

Rivets

Heart beating flutters
Chest opens full with colour
Bridge of two lovers
No need to check the rivets
We don't ever talk frigid.

Even Keel

Bless the joys of life such a lovely taste,
Sun rays shimmer as kisses skim the river,
The best I've known is this bliss that we chased,
Heart flutters chest opens full of colour;
From the inside you shape the perfect form;
The quality of beauty in design,
Dreaming walking under stars arm in arm,
Divine queen of the Earth one of a kind,
Perfume trails linger in elevation,
Heaven sent, clouds entangled breeze away,
Like a ship that sets sail on an ocean—
Of emotion on currents we ride waves,
The lamp burning doesn't last forever;
Handed down it's forever remembered.

Rainbow's End

My eye in the sky
Hides behind magic carpets
That trickle into
An Elysium harvest
Followed to a rainbow's end.

Thank you for reading the book. I would like to thank the energy of the Universe for its both instability and stability of producing life and the pleasure of observing such beauty in equilibrium. Thanks to my family, friends, and my dog R.I.P Nessi.

I would appreciate any feedback or questions - you are welcome to send me a message at spiritlevel333@gmail.com.

Printed in Great Britain
by Amazon